Summary

Congress has indicated a strong interest in ensuring that today's young people—those ages 16 through 24—attain the education and employment experience necessary to make the transition to adulthood as skilled workers and taxpayers. In the wake of the December 2007-June 2009 recession, questions remain about the employment prospects of youth today and the possible effects on their future earnings and participation in the labor market.

This report provides context for policymakers on the youth employment situation. It includes data on labor force participation, employment, and unemployment in the post-World War II period, with a focus on trends since 2000. This discussion compares rates based on age, gender, race/ethnicity, and income, where applicable. The report also explores the factors that influence youth participation in the labor force and their prospects for employment.

Major Findings

- Over the past decade, teens and young adults have experienced a precipitous decline in employment and a corresponding increase in unemployment. In 2000, their employment to population (E/P) ratio, or employment rate, was about 60%. Their E/P ratio steadily eroded even when the economy grew in the mid-2000s. The December 2007-June 2009 recession resulted in record low employment for this population. Since the official end of the recession, younger workers have continued to fare poorly in the labor market. In 2011, youth ages 16 through 24 had an E/P ratio of 45.5% and a rate of unemployment at 17.3%. This is compared to an employment rate of 75.1% and an unemployment rate of 7.9% for workers of prime working age, 25 through 54.

- Recent declining employment rates for young people are likely due to decreasing demand for labor generally and youth foregoing work for higher education. Youth may decide to pursue education because of dismal employment prospects and the growing need for more education to be successful in the labor market.

- Throughout the post-World War II period, the E/P ratio has been highest for white youth, followed by Hispanic youth. Black and Asian youth have been the least likely to be employed. For black youth, this is likely due to lower educational attainment. Lower rates of employment for Asian youth is likely attributable to their increasing participation in postsecondary education. Young black males in particular have had the lowest E/P ratios.

- Beginning in the 1970s, the E/P ratios for women increased as they entered the workforce in greater numbers. The gender difference in the E/P ratio for teens and young adults began to narrow in the 1990s, likely due to greater high school and college attainment among females and shifts in cultural expectations and public policies about women in the labor market.

- Lower employment rates—and simultaneous increases in unemployment—for young people appear to be due to a confluence of factors. Youth have less education and experience relative to older workers. During dips in economic activity, young adults may find it difficult to attain a first job, and are often most vulnerable to layoff because firms are more likely to lay off those with less seniority and less training.

- The consequences of decreasing E/P ratios and increasing unemployment among youth have not been fully explored. Preliminary research in this area has hypothesized that reductions in human capital, such as deterioration of skills and foregone work experience, may have lasting impacts on the employability and wages of youth. Some studies show that on average, early youth unemployment has negative effects on incomes but not as strong effects on future unemployment; however, youth entering the labor market during severe downturns in the economy appear to have relatively lower wages in the longer term.

Contents

Figures

Tables

Appendixes

Contacts

Introduction

This report provides current and historical employment and unemployment information about young people ages 16 through 24. It begins with a brief background on the December 2007-June 2009 recession and its lasting effects on youth currently in the labor force. It then discusses employment and education pathways that young people today can pursue. Following this section is a description of the labor market data used in the report. The report goes on to provide data on labor force participation, employment, and unemployment in the post-World War II period, with a focus on trends since 2000. This discussion compares rates based on age, gender, race/ethnicity, and income, where applicable. The report concludes by exploring the factors that influence the extent to which youth participate in the labor force and their prospects for employment. This last section also discusses the possible consequences of decreasing employment and increasing unemployment among youth. The **Appendix** includes supplemental tables and figures on the youth employment situation. The findings of the report are discussed in the summary.

Given the challenges that young people experience in the labor market, this report may be of interest to Congress in the context of workforce development, education, unemployment insurance, youth policy, or macroeconomic policy; however, the report does not discuss specific programs or policy implications.[1]

Background

Although the recession that began in December 2007 officially ended 18 months later, in June 2009, many workers were still struggling to find work, and continue to do so today. Unemployment since the recession has been as high as 9%. The recession exacerbated challenges that workers have faced in securing and retaining employment over the past decade, when the U.S. economy had the slowest job growth since 1940.[2] Coined "The Lost Decade" by some economists, 2000 through 2010 saw no net gains in jobs.[3] Against this backdrop, young people ages 16 through 24 have experienced the steepest decreases in employment.

Declines in the youth employment rate, or employment to population (E/P) ratio, and labor force participation may be due, in part, to overall weak demand for workers and growing youth enrollment in high school and postsecondary education. As discussed throughout this report, education is a protective factor for young workers: greater educational attainment is associated with higher wages and lower unemployment. Nonetheless, recent college graduates face dismal employment prospects in the wake of the 2007-2009 recession. Calling youth coming of age today "Generation Limbo" or "The Lost Generation," media reports chronicle recent college graduates who are unable to start their careers and instead are relying on their parents or public

---

[1] For further information about programs and policy responses, see CRS Report IS42176, *CRS Introductory Statement on Employment and Training Policy*, coordinated by David H. Bradley and CRS Report IS42239, *CRS Introductory Statement on Economic Recovery and Jobs*, coordinated by Linda Levine.

[2] Congressional Research Service (CRS), based on data from U.S. Department of Labor, Bureau of Labor Statistics (BLS), Current Employment Statistics (CES) Survey. The percent change in total nonfarm employment between the first and last year of the 1940s-2000s period by decade is as follows: 1940s, 35.3%; 1950s, 17.9%; 1960s, 29.9%; 1970s, 26.7%; 1980s, 19.3%; 1990s, 17.8%; 2000s, -1.5%.

[3] Neil Irwin, "Aughts were a Lost Decade for U.S. Economy, Workers," *Washington Post*, January 2, 2010.

benefits to get by.[4] Just over one quarter of recent college graduates (from the classes of 2006 through 2011) with jobs report that they are working below their education level, and about 43% of those said their jobs do not require a college degree. Further, 6 out of 10 recent college graduates believe that their generation will do less well than their parents' generation.[5]

Education and Employment Pathways for Young People

For the purposes of this report, *youth* refers to young people ages 16 through 24. Individuals as young as 16 are included because the Department of Labor's Bureau of Labor Statistics (BLS), which maintains official records of employment and unemployment, counts workers beginning at this age.[6] Although traditional definitions of youth have considered adolescence to be a period ending at age 18, cultural and economic shifts have protracted the time for youth to transition to adulthood. Older youth, up to age 24, are included because they are often still in school and/or living with their parents.[7] The current move from adolescence to adulthood has become longer and more complex, and policymakers and others are recognizing that adolescence is no longer a finite period that ends at the age of majority.[8]

Young people ages 16 through 24 may pursue a variety of education and employment pathways. Those of high school age may attend high school and/or work. Youth with a high school diploma can attend a two- or four-year college, enlist in the armed services, or secure part-time or full-time employment. Youth sometimes work and attend school simultaneously. Young people who drop out of high school can do some of these same things, but their opportunities are more limited. They cannot enroll in a four-year college or, in most cases, enlist in the military. They may also face challenges securing employment.[9]

Even young people who are attending high school or an institution of higher education (or those on a break from school) may still want to work, or feel that they have to work, for a variety of reasons—to have spending cash, contribute to their household income, gain work experience, and

---

[4] Hope Yen, "1 in 2 New College Grads Jobless or Underemployed," *The Associated Press*, April 24, 2012; Jennifer 8. Lee, "Generation Limbo: Waiting It Out," *New York Times*, August 31, 2011; and Adam Clark Estes, "More Signs That American Youth are a Lost Generation," *The Atlantic Wire*, September 22, 2011.

[5] About three quarters of respondents reported having at least one full-time job since graduation, with a median salary of $28,000. Charley Stone, Cliff Zukin, and Carl Van Horn, *Chasing the American Dream: Recent College Graduates and the Recent Recession*, Rutgers University, John J. Heldrich Center for Workforce Development, May 2012, http://www.heldrich rutgers.edu/sites/default/files/content/Chasing_American_Dream_Report.pdf.

[6] The Fair Labor Standards Act (FLSA) sets 14 years of age as the minimum age for employment and limits the number of hours worked by minors under the age of 16.

[7] Arguably, the age of youth could be even higher than 24. For example, the Patient Protection and Affordable Care Act (P.L. 111-148) uses the age of 26. Specifically, the law requires health insurance companies to provide coverage to the children of parents who are enrolled in their health care plans up to their 26th birthday. It also provides a new Medicaid pathway, effective January 2014, for children who age out of foster care up to their 26th birthday.

[8] For further information on the transition to adulthood, see CRS Report RL33975, *Vulnerable Youth: Background and Policies*, by Adrienne L. Fernandes-Alcantara.

[9] For further discussion, see CRS Report R40535, *Disconnected Youth: A Look at 16- to 24-Year Olds Who Are Not Working or In School*, by Adrienne L. Fernandes-Alcantara and Thomas Gabe. See also Gordon L. Berlin, Frank F. Furstenberg, Jr., and Mary C. Waters, "Introducing the Issue," *Future of Children Volume on the Transition to Adulthood*, vol. 20, no. 1 (Spring 2010), pp. 1-17.

---

save for the future, among other possibilities. In a nationally representative survey in 2005, nearly 7 out of 10 high school seniors reported that they expect work to be a central part of their lives, and almost 90% said they value a job that offers a reasonably predictable future.[10] About 80% reported that they valued a job that is intrinsically rewarding because it is interesting to do, uses one's skills and abilities, and allows one to learn new things, among other factors. Nearly the same percentage of seniors valued work because of its extrinsic rewards, including that a job— has high status and prestige that most people look up to and respect; allows for advancement and promotion; and provides one with a chance to earn a good deal of money.

Young people can more readily secure employment, especially employment that pays well, if they have some postsecondary education. As the level of education rises, the unemployment rate decreases and median weekly earnings increase for those who work. Among labor force participants without a high school diploma in 2010, the unemployment rate was 14.9%; this compares to an unemployment rate of 10.3% and 5.4% for those with a high school degree or a bachelor's degree, respectively (see **Figure 7** for further detail).[11] The Bureau of Labor Statistics (BLS) predicts that the fastest growing occupations between 2010 and 2020 will require postsecondary degrees.[12] Further, in all career clusters, a bachelor's degree or better offers accessibility to most high-paying jobs.[13] As discussed later in the report, the growing need for education to secure employment is likely a major reason why some young people are foregoing work for school. Still, BLS predicts that two-thirds of new jobs and 70% of job openings to replace workers will require only a high school diploma or less.

Overview of Data

This report uses BLS employment and unemployment data that are based on a household survey conducted by the Census Bureau. This survey, known as the Current Population Survey (CPS), collects labor force and other data from a nationally representative sample of 60,000 households. The survey includes households with civilian non-institutionalized individuals and excludes individuals residing in correctional facilities, residential nursing and mental health facilities, college dorms, military facilities, and other institutions. Employed and unemployed youth (beginning at age 16) and adults (no upper age limit) are counted by BLS as part of the *labor force*. The *labor force participation rate* is the percentage of individuals in the population who are employed and who are unemployed. People who are neither employed nor unemployed are not in the labor force.

---

[10] Laura Wray-Lake et al., "Exploring the Changing Meaning of Work for American High School Seniors From 1976 to 2005," *Youth & Society*, vol. 43, no. 3, 2011, pp. 1110-1135.

[11] U.S. Department of Labor, Bureau of Labor Statistics, Current Population Survey; *Education Pays*, May 2011, http://www.bls.gov/emp/ep_chart_001 htm.

[12] C. Brett Lockard and Michael Wolf, "Occupational Employment Projections to 2020," *Monthly Labor Review*, vol. 135, no. 1 (January 2012), pp. 88, 90, http://www.bls.gov/opub/mlr/2012/01/art5full.pdf. (Hereinafter, Lacey and Wright, "Occupational Employment Projections to 2018."). See also, Anthony P. Carnevale, Nicole Smith, and Jeff Strohl, *Help Wanted: Projections of Jobs and Education Requirements through 2018*, Georgetown University, Center on Education and the Workforce, June 2010, http://cew.georgetown.edu/JOBS2018/.

[13] Anthony P. Carnevale et al., *Career Cluster: Forecasting Demand for High School Through College Jobs 2008-2018*, November 2011, http://cew.georgetown.edu/clusters/.

BLS considers individuals to be *employed* if they work at all for pay or profit during the week that they are surveyed.[14] This includes all part-time and temporary work, as well as regular full-time, year-round employment. It does not include unpaid internships. Individuals are still counted as employed if they have a job at which they did not work during the survey week, even if they were not paid, because they were on vacation, experiencing child care problems, on maternity or paternity leave, or some other reason. The employment rate, or the *employment to population (E/P) ratio*, is the proportion of individuals in the general U.S. population who are employed. Individuals are considered *unemployed* if they are in the labor force and are jobless, looking for jobs, and available for work. Job search activities include sending out resumes or filling out applications, among other activities. The *unemployment rate* is the share of individuals in the labor force who are unemployed (note that the denominator for the E/P ratio and the unemployment rate are different).[15]

Labor market participation by youth, as well as adults, is a proxy indicator of interest in working. Generally, increasing labor force participation indicates greater interest in working, while decreasing labor force participation indicates declining or noninterest in working. Changes in labor force participation rates, however, are not perfect indicators of individual or collective interest in working. For example, labor force participation may decline because individuals become discouraged about job prospects and give up looking for work. Individuals may also decide to pursue education instead because of the returns they will receive later when they are employed.

The E/P ratio and the unemployment rate can help to gauge market conditions. A stable and high E/P ratio suggests that the economy is healthy, in that individuals are able to find employment. The unemployment rate is also an indicator of whether individuals are able to be employed in the labor force. This rate should be interpreted with caution: changes in the unemployment rate can mask the extent to which individuals want to work. The unemployment rate may decline when firms are not hiring because individuals become discouraged and drop out of the labor market.

In addition to the official count of unemployment, BLS records the number of people who are not in the labor force. Some individuals out of the labor force indicate that they want a job. Those who want a job are *marginally attached* to the labor force if they searched for work during the past 12 months and were available to take a job but had not looked for work in the past four weeks. Marginally attached workers are considered *discouraged* if they did not look for work for one or more of the following reasons: they thought that no work was available, could not find work, lacked the requisite schooling or training, or faced age or other types of discrimination. Marginally attached workers may also be unable to work for such reasons as school or family responsibilities, ill health, and transportation, as well other reasons for which nonparticipation could not be determined.

---

[14] BLS also counts workers who are "unpaid family workers," which includes any person who worked without pay for 15 hours or more per week in a family-owned enterprise operated by someone in their household. Unpaid family workers comprise a relatively small proportion of total employment.

[15] The unemployment rate is the number of unemployed individuals / (employed + unemployed individuals in the labor force) and the employment rate, or employment to population ratio is the number of employed individuals / civilian non-institutionalized population).

Recent Trends

Both the E/P ratio and the unemployment rate provide a snapshot of how well youth are faring in the labor market. **Table 1** provides these and other relevant labor force data for individuals ages 16 and older and by age groups—youth ages 16 through 19 ("teens"), youth ages 20 through 24 ("young adults"), and other age groups (through age 69) in 2011. The table shows that for workers generally, the labor participation rate was 64.1% and the unemployment rate was 8.9%. In addition, nearly 6 out of 10 individuals in the population overall were employed.

Except for the oldest individuals, teens had the lowest rates of labor force participation (34.1%) and employment (25.8%), and the highest rate of unemployment (24.4%). While young adults participated at a high rate in the labor force (71.3%), they also experienced a relatively high rate of unemployment (14.6%). Individuals of prime working age (25 through 54) had the highest rates of labor force participation (81.6%) and employment (75.1%) and the lowest rate of unemployment (7.9%). Those ages 55 through 64 had a relatively average level of employment (60.3%) and the lowest rate of unemployment (6.6%) among the featured age groups. The oldest individuals in the table, those ages 65 through 69, had the lowest rate of labor force participation (32.1%), reflecting a high likelihood of retirement (and ability to receive Social Security benefits), and a relatively low unemployment rate (6.9%).

Table 1 also displays the share of individuals not in the labor force who wanted a job. Overall, 7.5% of workers not in the labor force wanted a job compared to 10% of teens and 15% of young adults. Approximately 3% of individuals not in the labor force were marginally attached, meaning that they were available for work within the past year but had not looked for a position within the past month (not shown in the table). A slightly greater share of teens (3.2%) and young adults (6.4%) were marginally attached. About 1% of all individuals (ages 16 and older) not in the labor force were discouraged. Teens and young adults were less likely than their older counterparts of any age group to report being discouraged. Of the reasons given for being discouraged, teens and young adults most frequently reported that they were not able to find work, followed by the belief that no work was available. These same two reasons were also most frequently reported for discouraged workers overall.[16]

Additional research indicates that young people want to work despite relatively low levels of labor force participation. The Center for Labor Market Studies estimated that the number of underutilized teens ages 16 through 19 was 2.8 million in the fourth quarter of 2009 (approximately two calendar quarters after the end of the recession).[17] This included individuals who would have liked to work but were not currently looking and who were employed part-time but would have preferred full-time work. This is in addition to the approximately 1.5 million youth counted as unemployed at the time. According to this analysis, a substantially larger number of youth would have liked to work than the official unemployment rate indicates.

[16] This is based on unpublished data provided to the Congressional Research Service by the U.S. Department of Labor, Bureau of Labor Statistics, March 2012.

[17] Andrew Sum and Ishwar Khatiwada, *Dire Straits in the Nation's Teen Labor Market: The Outlook for the Summer 2010 Teen Job Market and the Case for A Comprehensive Youth Jobs Creation Strategy*, Center for Labor Market Studies, April 2010.

Table 1. Labor Force Participation by Selected Age Groups, 2011

Numbers in thousands, not seasonally adjusted

Age Group	Civilian Non-institutionalized Population	Labor Force Participation Rate	E/P Ratio	Unemployment Rate	Percentage Not in the Labor Force Who Want Job
16-24	38,198	55.0%	45.5%	17.3%	11.8%
16-19	16,774	34.1	25.8	24.4	10.0
20-24	17,201	71.3	60.8	14.6	15.0
25-54	124,704	81.6	75.1	7.9	8.1
55-64	36,987	64.3	60.3	6.6	6.2
65-69	12,546	32.1	29.9	6.9	Not available
All	239,618	64.1	58.4	8.9	7.5

Source: Congressional Research Service (CRS), based on published and unpublished data from the U.S. Department of Labor, Bureau of Labor Statistics (BLS), Current Population Survey (CPS).

Note: All workers includes workers age 16 and older. The *labor force participation rate* is the percentage of individuals in the population who are employed and who are unemployed (those who are not employed and not looking for work are out of the labor force). The *E/P ratio* represents the percentage of the non-institutionalized population who are employed. The *unemployment rate* is the percentage of individuals in the labor force who are jobless, looking for jobs, and available for work. The share of persons not in the labor force includes individuals who have looked for work within the past year and those who have not.

Changes Since 2000

Table 2 displays the youth labor force participation rates, E/P ratios, and unemployment rates for all youth by gender and race/ethnicity in three recent years: 2000, 2007, and 2011. These three years are notable because they include a period when the economy was expanding (2000), a period just before the start of the recent recession (2007), and a period after the recession had officially ended (2011). Labor force trends for youth ages 16 through 24 were bleak even before the onset of the recession. From 2000 to 2007, the youth labor force participation decreased from 65.8% to 59.4%; their E/P ratio fell from 59.7% to 53.1%; and their unemployment rate increased from 9.3% to 10.5%.

From 2000 to 2011, the youth labor force participation rate decreased by about 16%: 65.8% of youth were in the labor force in 2000, compared to 55.0% in 2011. More youth dropped out of the labor force due likely to downward trends in the economy and the growing importance of education. A greater share of males than females left the labor force over this period. Minority youth—black, Hispanic, and Asian—were less likely than their white counterparts to be in the labor force. Asian youth had the lowest rates of labor force participation in both 2000 and 2011. As discussed later in this report, it appears that their E/P ratios reflect their greater likelihood of pursuing higher education in lieu of work compared with their racial/ethnic counterparts. Further, these trends do not persist among prime-age workers. Unlike other minority workers, Asian adults 25 through 54 had rates of employment (75%) comparable to those of their white counterparts (77%) in 2011.

Also over the 12-year period, the E/P ratio for 16-to-24 year olds decreased from 59.7% to 45.5%, a decline of about 14 percentage points. While more males than females were employed in both 2000 and 2011, males experienced greater declines in their E/P ratio. Employment for all racial/ethnic groups decreased by 10 to 15 percentage points. White and Hispanic youth had the most dramatic decreases, with the white E/P ratio decreasing from 64.5% to 48.6% and the Hispanic E/P ratio decreasing from 57.6% to 42.2%. However, black and Asian youth had the lowest E/P ratios in both years. About 34% of black youth and 36% of Asian youth were employed in 2011, compared to about 46% for each group in 2000.

Further, the unemployment rate for youth nearly doubled over the 2000-2011 period, with an increase from 9.3% to 17.3% (total unemployment for all workers also almost doubled over this period). In both 2000 and 2011, males were more likely to be unemployed than females. About 3 out of 10 (29.0%) black youth were unemployed in 2011. This is compared to a 2011 unemployment rate of 15.3% for white youth, 19.4% for Hispanic youth, and 14.0% for Asian youth.

Notably the *relative* change in the labor force participation rate and E/P ratio was constant for each racial/ethnic group over time; however, the relative change in the unemployment rate varied significantly by race/ethnicity. Black and Asian youth experienced the smallest relative change in unemployment at about 54% to 56%, whereas the unemployment rate more than doubled for white youth and almost doubled for Hispanic youth.

Table A-1 and **Table A-2** in the **Appendix** include labor force participation rates, E/P ratios, and unemployment rates for youth ages 16-to-19 and 20-to-24 in 2000, 2007, and 2011. From 2000 to 2011, teens saw striking declines in their labor force participation (-34.4%) and E/P ratios (-43.3%) compared to young adults (-8.4% and -15.8%, respectively). While teen unemployment was higher, the *relative* change in unemployment for young adults was greater. The teen unemployment rate almost doubled and the young adult unemployment rate more than doubled.

Table 2. Labor Force Trends of Youth Ages 16-24 by Gender and Race/Ethnicity: 2000, 2007, and 2011

Numbers in thousands, not seasonally adjusted

	2000	2007	2011	Absolute Change from 2000-2011 (Percentage Points)[a]	Relative Change from 2000-2011 (Percentage)[a]
Labor Force Participation Rate					
All	65.8	59.4	55.0	-10.8	-16.4
Male	68.6	61.5	56.6	-12.0	-17.5
Female	63.0	57.2	53.3	-9.7	-15.4
White	69.7	62.0	57.3	-12.4	-17.8
Black	56.1	50.2	47.8	-8.3	-14.8
Hispanic	64.3	57.9	52.4	-11.9	-18.5
Asian	50.5	45.1	41.4	-9.1	-18.0

	2000	2007	2011	Absolute Change from 2000-2011 (Percentage Points)a	Relative Change from 2000-2011 (Percentage)a
E/P Ratio					
All	59.7	53.1	45.5	-14.2	-23.8
Male	61.9	54.4	46.0	-15.9	-25.7
Female	57.4	51.8	44.9	-12.5	-21.8
White	64.5	56.3	48.6	-15.9	-24.7
Black	45.7	40.5	33.9	-11.8	-25.8
Hispanic	57.6	51.7	42.2	-15.4	-26.7
Asian	45.9	41.9	35.6	-10.3	-22.4
Unemployment Rate					
All	9.3	10.5	17.3	8.0	86.0
Male	9.7	11.6	18.7	9.0	92.8
Female	8.9	9.4	15.7	6.8	76.4
White	7.4	9.2	15.3	7.9	106.8
Black	18.5	19.3	29.0	10.5	56.8
Hispanic	10.4	10.7	19.4	9.0	86.5
Asian	9.1	7.2	14.0	4.9	53.8

Source: Congressional Research Service (CRS), based on data from U.S. Department of Labor, Bureau of Labor Statistics, Current Population Survey,

Notes: The labor force participation rate is the percentage of individuals in the population who are employed and unemployed (those who are not employed and not looking for work are out of the labor force). Employment-population ratios represent the percentage of the non-institutionalized population who were employed. The unemployment rate is the percentage of individuals in the labor force who are jobless, looking for jobs, and available for work. Persons of Hispanic origin can be of any race and individuals of any race may be Hispanic.

a. Absolute change refers to the percentage point change from 2000 to 2011, and is derived by subtracting 2011 data from 2000 data. Relative change refers to the percentage change over the same period, and is derived by subtracting 2011 data from 2000 data and then dividing that number by the 2000 data.

Unemployment and the 2007-2009 Recession

The 18-month recession that spanned December 2007 through June 2009, sometimes called "the Great Recession," disproportionately affected young people. **Figure 1** shows the seasonally adjusted unemployment rates for teens, young adults, and adults of prime working age from the fourth quarter of 2007 through the fourth quarter of 2011. Over this period, unemployment rates for all groups steadily increased for each age cohort, peaking in 2009. Teen unemployment climbed from 16.1% at the end of 2007 to 26.8% at the end of 2009. During these same two years, the unemployment rate for young adults increased significantly, almost doubling from 8.7% in the fourth quarter of 2007 to 15.8% in the fourth quarter of 2009. Notably, the unemployment rates for teens increased over the first three quarters of 2011, and then declined (to 23.6%) in the fourth quarter. The unemployment rates for young adults and workers of prime age declined over the four quarters in 2011, but these rates were higher than they were in 2007 and 2008.

Figure 1. Quarterly Unemployment Rates by Select Age Groups, Fourth Quarter of 2007 through Fourth Quarter of 2011

Seasonally adjusted

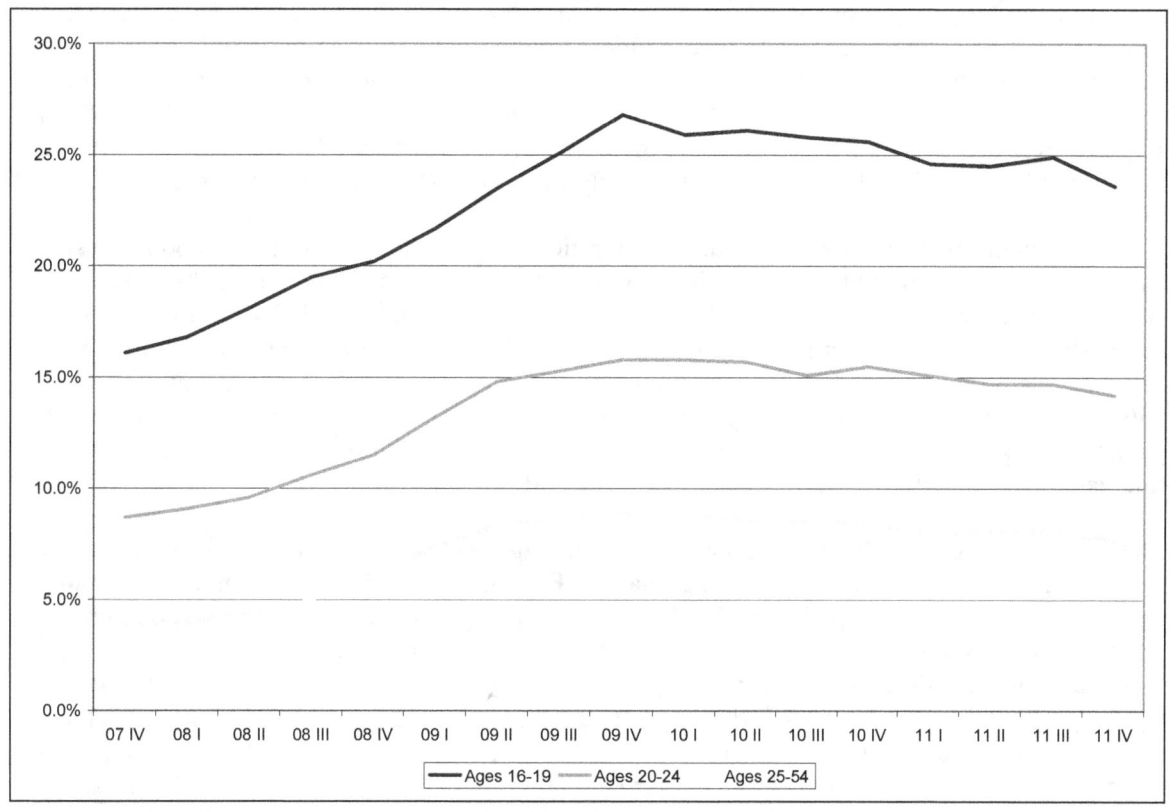

Source: Congressional Research Service (CRS), based on data from U.S. Department of Labor, Bureau of Labor Statistics, Current Population Survey.

Notes: The unemployment rate is the percentage of individuals in the labor force who are jobless, looking for jobs, and available for work.

Trends Over Time

The figures and tables in the remainder of the report include employment and unemployment data over the period following World War II based on age, gender, race/ethnicity, and family income.[18]

Age

The labor market experiences of youth are different based on their age. **Figure 2** shows the E/P ratio from 1948 through 2011 for teens, young adults, and adults ages 25 through 54. (The figure

---

[18] The data are not seasonally adjusted, meaning that they have not been adjusted to account for seasonality in employment and unemployment rates.

also displays the 11 periods when the country was in recession.[19]) Over that time, teens had the lowest rates of employment, while adults of prime working age had the highest employment rates.

Youth

The E/P ratio for teens was 47.7% in 1948 and reached a post-World War II low of 25.8% in 2011. In the intervening years, there was variation in the rate—with 42.0% as the average. The data show points at which E/P ratios reached local troughs and peaks. As expected, teen employment generally declined soon after the start of a recession and reached local lows at the end of the recession or a year or two later. Notably, the teen employment rate was below 40% in 17 years over this 64-year period. Seven of those years were between 1958 and 1965 and 10 were between 2002 through 2011. This suggests a fairly recent long-term decline in teen employment.

Also over the post-World War II period, the E/P ratio for young adults was higher and more stable than it was for teens. In both 1948 and 2011, approximately 6 out of 10 young adults were employed. Unlike the teen E/P ratio, which had more cyclical trends, the E/P ratio for young adults steadily improved over the period, particularly following the 1960-1961 recession. This could be due, in part, to women entering the labor market in greater numbers starting in the 1960s. Declines in the E/P ratios for young adults over the entire period were fairly small. The greatest change to the E/P ratio for this population occurred in the last decade, when the rate fluctuated from a high of 72.2% in 2000 to a low of 60.3% in 2010.

The long-term decline in employment rates for youth ages 16 to 19 appears to reflect, at least in some part, their withdrawal from the labor market. **Figure A-1** and **Figure A-2** in the **Appendix** show the labor force participation rate, E/P ratio, and unemployment rate for teens and young adults from 1948 through 2011. Over this period, labor force participation for teens was lower than that of young adults. Teen labor force participation trended upward from the 1960s until reaching a peak in 1979 at nearly 58%. Over the next two decades, the rate was uneven. It then declined by about one-third from 2000 to 2011. In contrast to teens, the labor force participation of young adults steadily increased in most years over the post-World War II period. It was stable at about 70% to 80% in most years; however, at the start of the 2000s it began to tick downward, reaching its lowest point (in 2010) since the early 1970s.

These changes can likely be viewed as partially a consequence of a positive social trend—the increase in school enrollment, particularly for youth ages 16-19.[20] In addition, as discussed later in the report, students are increasingly pursuing unpaid internships to meet high school graduation requirements and improve their prospects for attending college. So although they are gaining employment experience, they are not included in the labor force.

---

[19] These periods are November 1948 (IV) to October 1949 (IV); July 1953 (II) to May 1954 (II); August 1957 (III) to April 1958 (II); April 1960 (II) to February 1961 (I); December 1969 (IV) to November 1970 (IV); November 1973 (IV) to March 1975 (I); January 1980 (I) to July 1980 (III); July 1981 (III) to November 1982 (IV); July 1990 (III) to March 1991 (I); March 2001 (I) to November 2001 (IV); and December 2007 (IV) to June 2009 (II). See National Bureau of Economic Research, "U.S. Business Cycle Expansions and Contractions," http://www.nber.org/cycles/cyclesmain.html.

[20] U.S. Department of Education, National Center for Education Statistics, *Digest of Education Statistics 2009*, "Total fall enrollment in degree-granting institutions, by sex, age, and attendance status: Selected years, 1970 through 2018," April 2010.

Nonetheless, these trends do not necessarily reflect a tendency toward voluntary withdrawal from the workforce to complete schooling. Indeed, some young people may have dropped out of the labor market because of dismal employment prospects, especially in light of the jobless recovery following the 2001 recession. Although the economy rebounded, the E/P ratios of teens and young adults stabilized or declined in subsequent years. The 2007-2009 recession likely further contributed to the downward trend. The growing unemployment rate since the early 2000s suggests that some youth have withdrawn from the labor force because of their inability to find work. **Figure A-1** and **Figure A-2** in the **Appendix** show the unemployment rate for teens and young adults. The unemployment rate for teens was between 10% and 20% in most years over the post-World War II period. In 2010, this rate reached a recorded high of 25.9%. Only in five other years—1982, 1983, 1992, 2009, and 2011—did the teen unemployment rate exceed 20%. Notably, the E/P ratio and unemployment rate for teens converged in 2010 so that about one-quarter of teens in the general population were working and one-quarter of teens in the labor force were unemployed.

The unemployment trend line for young adults fluctuated over the post-war period, from a low of 4.1% in 1951 to a high of 15.5% in 2010 (and it improved to 14.6% in 2011). The last time unemployment increased above 11% for young adults was during the back-to-back recessions of the early 1980s, when the unemployment rate reached a high of 14.9% (in 1982).

Though not displayed, the unemployment rate for young black males was especially high over this same period—with an annual average of 36.5% for black teen males and 21.7% for black young adult males.[21] The average annual difference in unemployment rates was about 20 percentage points for black and white teen males and 12 percentage points for black and white young adult males.

Workers of Prime Age

As shown in **Figure 2**, the employment trend line for prime-age workers 25 through 54 was the highest of the three age groups. Although it was mostly parallel to the employment trend line for 20- through 24-year olds, older workers increasingly were more likely to be employed over time. From the 1950s through 1970s, workers of prime-age had somewhat comparable E/P ratios to young adults, with about 5% more prime-age workers employed in most years on average. Starting in the 1980s, the difference in their E/P ratios began to grow. By the 1990s, about 10% more of the prime-age population was employed than of the young adult population. This difference increased to 14% by 2011.

---

[21] Congressional Research Service (CRS) analysis based on data from U.S. Department of Labor, Bureau of Labor Statistics, Current Population Survey. Young Hispanic teen males also had higher rates of unemployment than white males; the rates for young adult Hispanic males and Asian male youth were comparable to the rates for their white counterparts.

Figure 2. Employment-Population Ratios by Select Age Groups, 1948-2011

Not seasonally adjusted

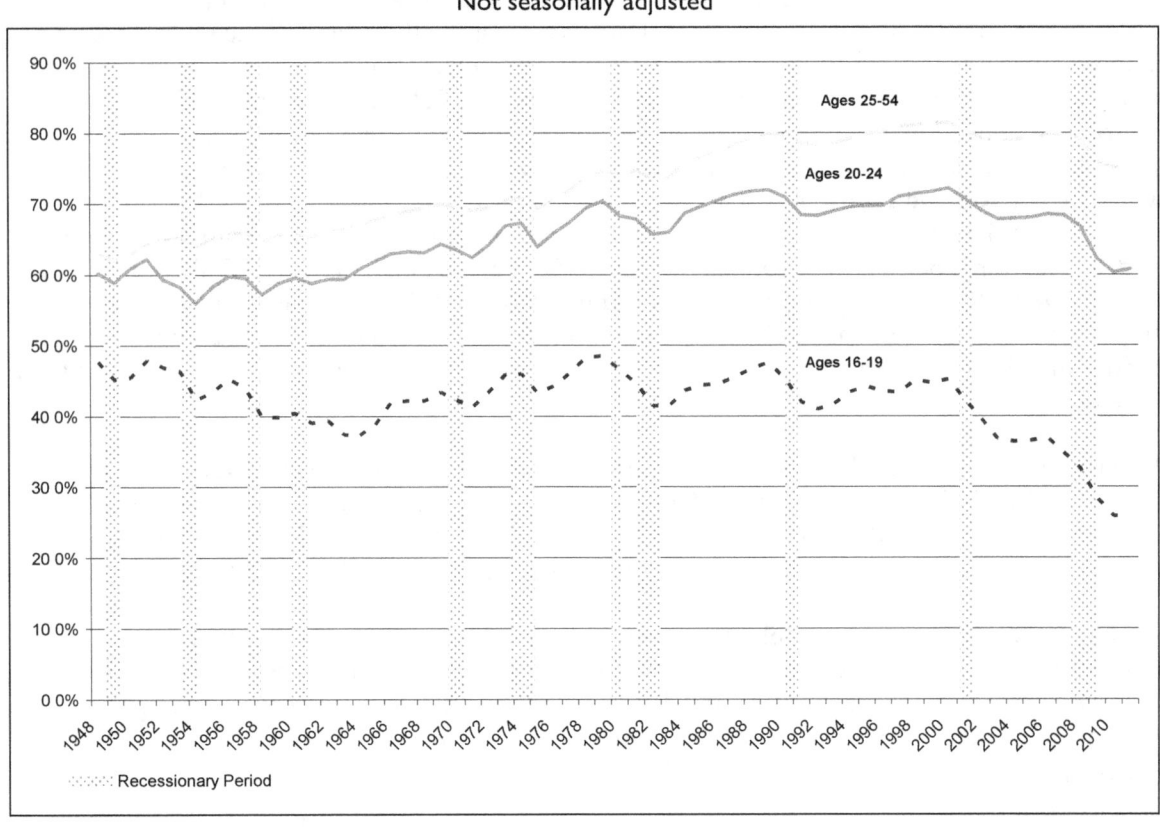

Source: Congressional Research Service (CRS), based on data from U.S. Department of Labor, Bureau of Labor Statistics, Current Population Survey.

Notes: Employment-population ratios represent the percentage of the non-institutionalized population who were employed.

Gender

The employment experiences of teens and young adults have differed based on gender. **Figure 3** shows the E/P ratios for female and male teens and young adults for 1948 through 2011. For many years, the E/P ratios for females were much lower than they were for their male counterparts; however, beginning in the mid-1960s, the E/P ratios for females, particularly young women, turned upward whereas the ratios for males tended to be downward trending. This was due, in part, to increasing numbers of women entering the labor force.[22] At this time, women began completing college at a higher rate than previous generations of women,[23] which may have influenced the extent to which they pursued and secured employment. In addition, cultural and

---

[22] From 1948 to 1978, the labor force participation of teen females increased by 11 percentage points from 42.0% to 53.7%. It peaked at 53.9% in 1989 and remained between 49% and 51% until the 2000s, when it began to decline and ultimately reached less than 40% in some subsequent years. Also from 1948 to 1978, the labor force participation of young adult females increased by 23 percentage points from 45.3% to 68.3%. It peaked at 73.2% in 1999 and decreased slightly in subsequent years.

[23] U.S. Census Bureau, "Percent of People 25 Years and Over Who Have Completed High School or College, by Race, Hispanic Origin and Sex: Selected Years 1940 to 2011." See data on young adults ages 25 through 29.

policy shifts (Title VII of the Civil Rights Act of 1964, as amended) were underway that encouraged women to enter the labor force. The difference in the E/P ratios for males and females in both age groups began to narrow in the 1990s, but likely for different reasons. For teens, the male E/P ratios started to drop while the female E/P ratios began to rise, so that by 1996 the rates were nearly identical. For young adults, females made significant inroads into the labor market. By the 1990s, their E/P ratios were similar to those of young males.

In most years since 2000, the E/P ratios of teen and young adult males and females declined. These declines were greater for male teens, such that the female teen E/P ratio surpassed that of males. The E/P ratio for young adult females was nearly the same as for young adult males in the past few years. These more recent shifts in the E/P ratios may be attributable to the changing employment prospects of less-educated individuals, as discussed further below. Young males ages 16 through 24 are somewhat less likely to be enrolled in high school or college than their female counterparts,[24] and a smaller share of males ages 25 through 29 have obtained a college degree.[25] Overall, young males had more negative labor market outcomes than females. As shown previously in **Table 2**, males were more likely to be unemployed over the past decade.

---

[24] The statistics are available in the following age categories: 16 and 17, 18 and 19, 20 and 21, and 22 to 24. For each of these age categories, females are more likely than males to be enrolled in school, particularly among those ages 18 through 21. U.S. Department of Education, National Center for Education Statistics, *Digest of Education Statistics: 2010*, Table 6, "Percentage of the Population 3 to 34 Years Old Enrolled In School, by Sex, Race/Ethnicity, and Age: Selected years, 1980 through 2009," July 2010, http://nces.ed.gov/programs/digest/d10/tables/dt10_006.asp?referrer=list.

[25] U.S. Census Bureau, "Percent of People 25 Years and Over Who Have Completed High School or College, by Race, Hispanic Origin and Sex: Selected Years 1940 to 2011."

Figure 3. Employment-Population Ratios of Teens and Young Adults by Gender, 1948-2011

Not seasonally adjusted

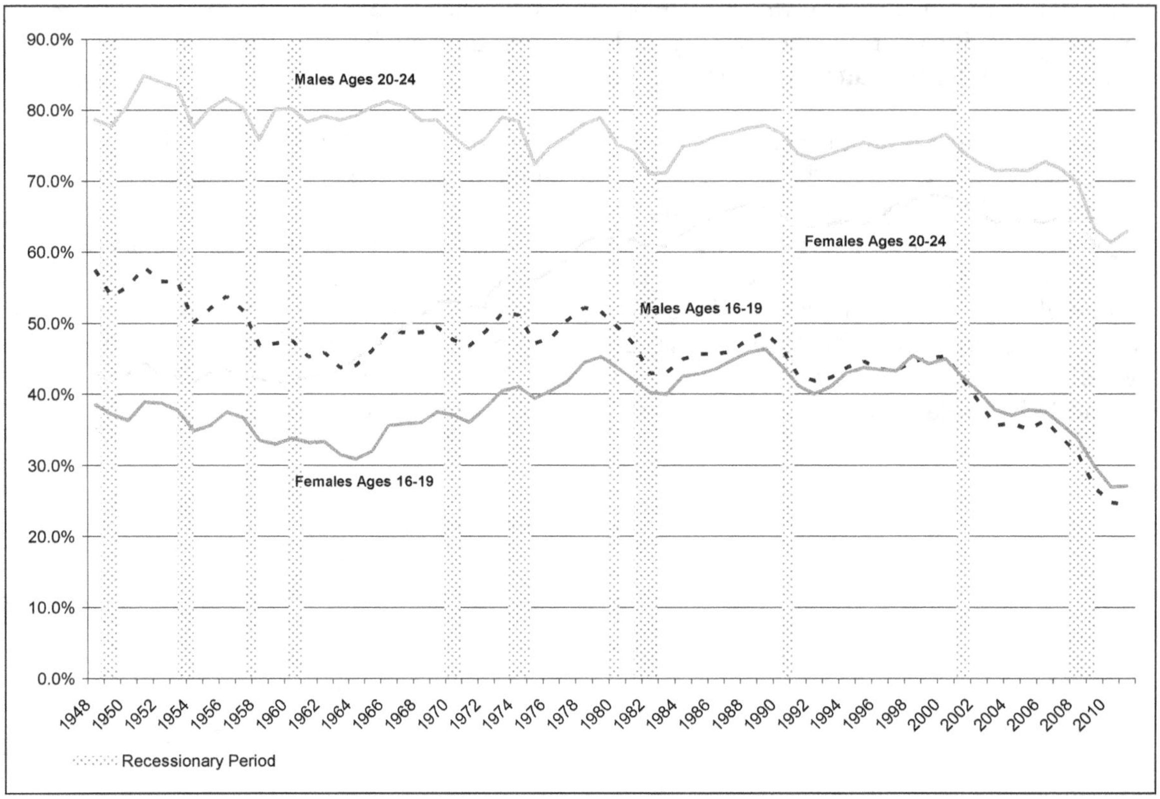

Source: Congressional Research Service (CRS), based on data from U.S. Department of Labor, Bureau of Labor Statistics, Current Population Survey.

Notes: Employment-population ratios represent the percentage of the non-institutionalized population who were employed.

Race and Ethnicity

Youth employment has also varied by race and ethnicity. Data on the E/P ratios of white youth have been available since 1954. The data for black, Hispanic, and Asian youth became available in 1972, 1994, and 2000, respectively. Over time, the E/P ratio was highest for white youth, followed by Hispanic youth. The E/P ratios for black and Asian youth were lower and somewhat comparable, with either group having the lowest employment depending on the year.

Figure 4 shows the E/P ratio of teens ages 16 to 19 by race and ethnicity. The employment trends for all groups reflected cyclical effects of the economy over the period depicted, until the late 1990s. Shortly thereafter, the E/P ratios for all groups declined by about 15 to 20 percentage points, with white teens having the steepest decline in employment over the period of recovery following the 2000 recession. **Figure 5** shows the employment trends for young adults by race and ethnicity. Employment for white young adults steadily increased, even during most recessions over the post-World War II period. In 1954, their E/P ratio was 55.9%, and in 2000 it peaked at 75.2%. It then declined steadily, reaching a recent low of 63.8% in 2010.

Still, minority youth had the lowest rates of employment relative to white youth. The lower rates of employment among minority youth may be due, in part, to the fewer employment prospects of individuals with less education (see discussion below). Overall, African Americans and Hispanics ages 16 through 24 are less likely to have completed high school and college.[26] Schooling may also explain the relatively low E/P ratios for Asian youth, but for a different reason. Asian youth have had the highest rates of school completion for college (and comparable rates for high school completion compared to white youth). Further, as shown in **Table 2**, Asian youth had the lowest rates of unemployment in recent years, which is likely a reflection of their high rates of school attainment.

**Figure 4. Employment-Population Ratio of Teens Ages 16-19
by Race and Ethnicity, 1954-2011**

Not seasonally adjusted

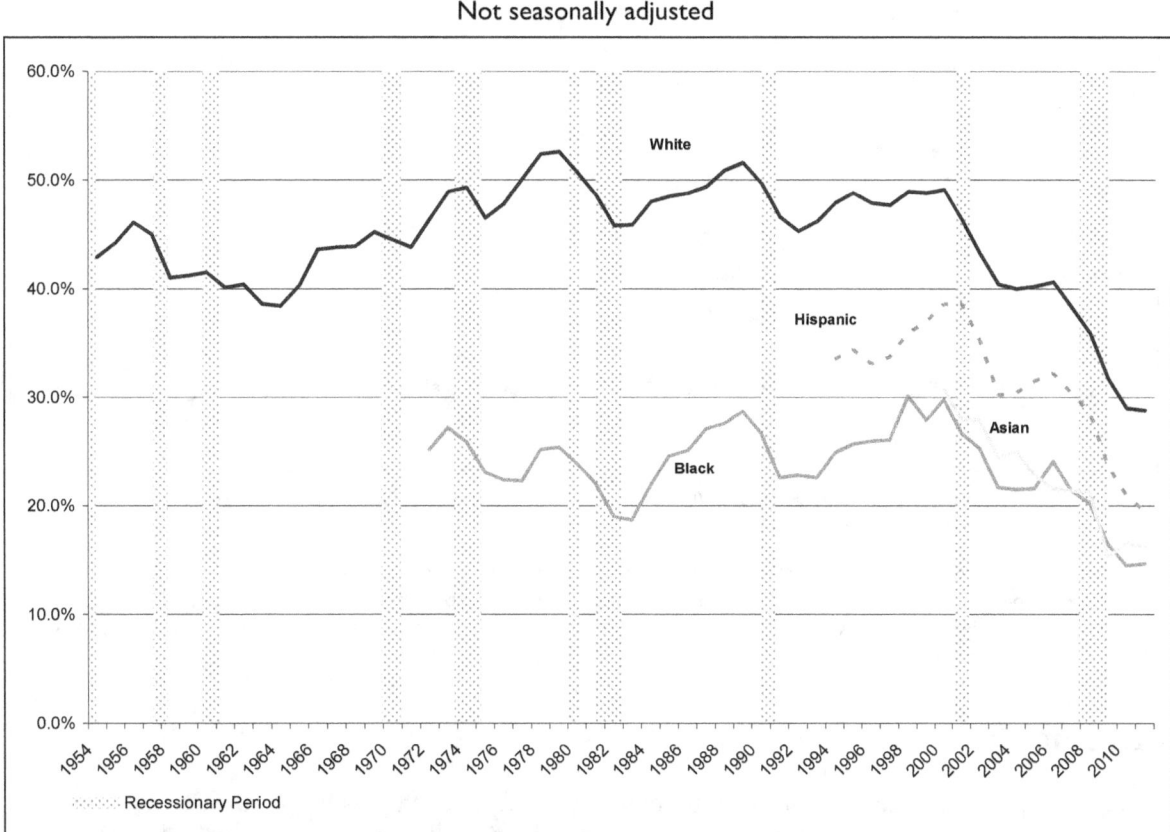

Source: Congressional Research Service (CRS), based on data from U.S. Department of Labor, Bureau of Labor Statistics, Current Population Survey.

Notes: Employment-population ratios represent the percentage of the non-institutionalized population who were employed. The Bureau of Labor Statistics began recording employment data for blacks in 1972, for Hispanics in 1994, and for Asians in 2000. Persons of Hispanic origin can be of any race and individuals of any race may be Hispanic.

---

[26] U.S. Department of Commerce, Census Bureau, Annual Social and Economic Supplement to the Current Population Survey, Table A-2, "Percent of People 25 Years and Over Who Have Completed High School or College, by Race, Hispanic Origin and Sex: Selected Years 1940 to 2011," http://www.census.gov/hhes/socdemo/education/data/cps/historical/index html. (Hereinafter, Census Bureau, "Percent of People 25 Years and Over Who Have Completed High School or College, by Race, Hispanic Origin and Sex: Selected Years 1940 to 2011.")

**Figure 5. Employment-Population Ratio of Young Adults Ages 20-24
by Race and Ethnicity, 1954-2011**

Not seasonally adjusted

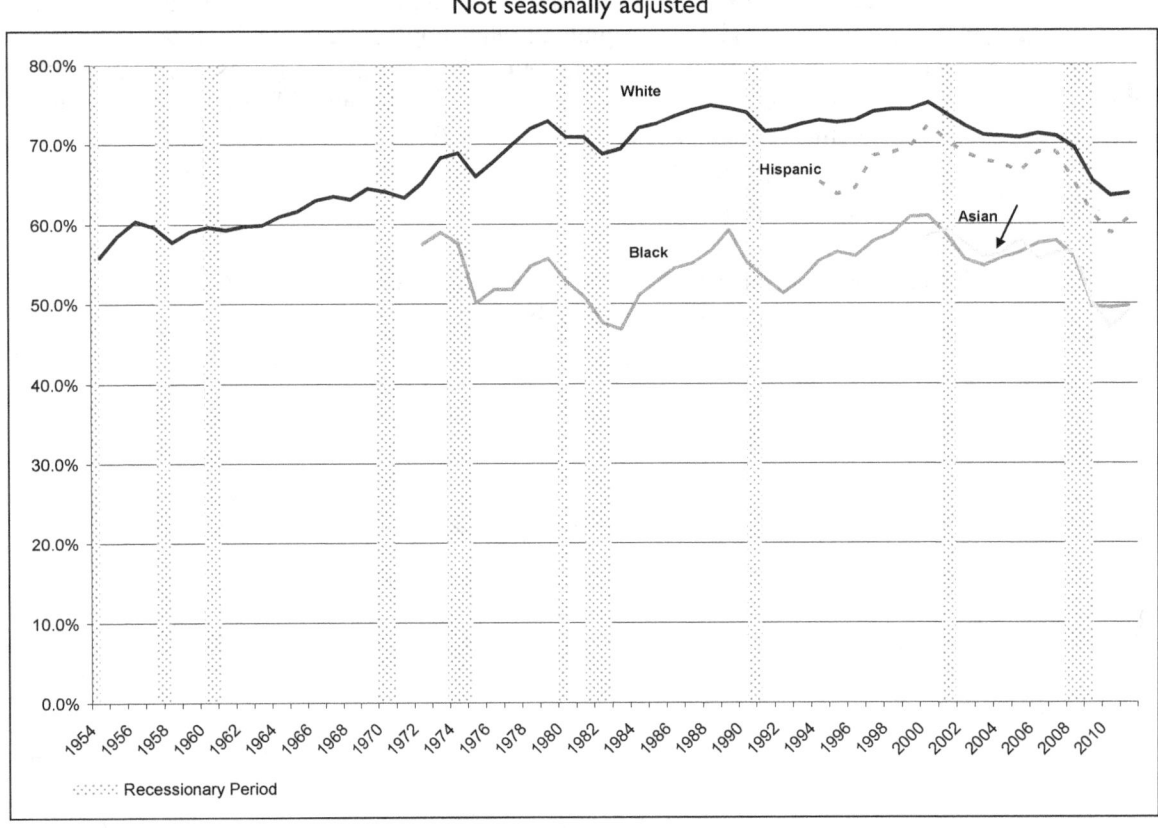

Source: Congressional Research Service (CRS) based on data from U.S. Department of Labor, Bureau of Labor Statistics, Current Population Survey.

Notes: Employment-population ratios represent the percentage of the non-institutionalized population who were employed. The Bureau of Labor Statistics began recording employment data for blacks in 1972, for Hispanics in 1994, and for Asians in 2002. Persons of Hispanic origin can be of any race and individuals of any race may be Hispanic.

Income

Finally, employment rates tend to vary by family income. An analysis by Northeastern University's Center for Labor Studies shows the summer employment rate of teens ages 16 through 19 increases as household income increases.[27] In 2011, about one out of every five teens in households with earnings below $20,000 worked, compared to about one-third of teens with household incomes of $40,000 to $60,000 or $60,000 to $75,000, and 37.2% of teens in households with incomes of $75,000 to $100,000. The association between family income and employment rates was positive but not quite as strong for white and Hispanic teens. Only among Asian youth was there no positive relationship between family income and summer employment. The author explained that while further research is needed on the association between family

---

[27] Andrew Sum, Iswhar Khatiwada, and Sheila Palma, *The Continued Collapse of the Nation's Teen Summer Job Market: Who Worked in the Summer of 2011?*, Center for Labor Market Studies, Northeastern University, September 2011, http://www.northeastern.edu/clms/wp-content/uploads/August-Summer-Job-Report.pdf.

income and youth employment, other studies have shown that parents of affluent teens often value work among their teenage children to encourage socialization and to take on adult roles. In addition, families in which both parents work can assist teens access jobs through their own networks whereas low-income teens tend to have fewer employed parents and may live with only one parent.

The research literature has not explored the extent to which low-income youth pursue employment because of their family's financial situation. While youth may want to work, they may choose not to because of the possibility that their families would lose eligibility for assistance programs. For example, the income of youth under age 18 who are in school is not counted as part of household income under the federal Supplemental Nutrition Assistance Program (SNAP) program (formerly known as the Food Stamp program).[28] This appears to mean that the income of those youth under age 18 who are not in school and any youth age 18 and older is included as household income.[29] In the Department of Housing and Urban Development (HUD)'s rental assistance programs, income is defined as income from all sources from all members of the household; however, this excludes income from children under age 18 and any earnings in excess of $480 for full-time students age 18 and older (unless the student is the head of household or spouse).[30] Therefore, the income of youth age 18 and older who are part-time students or are working would count. Nonetheless, not all federal assistance programs, such as Head Start[31] and Temporary Assistance for Needy Families (TANF),[32] systematically count youth's income as household income.

Factors Influencing the Youth Employment Situation

The decrease in the youth E/P ratio is associated with increasing youth unemployment. Both of these indicators demonstrate that the labor market for youth is at historic lows in terms of opportunity. There are many factors that affect labor market outcomes for youth; several factors affect the labor market as a whole and some are more specific to youth. This section provides a brief summary of some of these factors.

The Labor Market

One likely explanation of the dismal employment opportunities for youth is the supply of jobs and demand for workers. In general, firms lay off workers during recessions to respond to reduced demand for their goods and services. In the latest recession, which started in late 2007, the decline in economic activity (as measured by gross domestic product, or GDP) bottomed out

---

[28] 7 USC §2014(d)(7) and 7 CFR 273.9(c)(7).

[29] The program includes income earned in programs funded under Title I of the Workforce Investment Act, except if this income is earned by a dependent under age 18. See 7 USC §2014(l).

[30] 24 C.F.R. §5.609(c)(1) and 24 C.F.R. §5.609(c)(11).

[31] Office of Head Start Program Clarification OHS-PC-I-011, April 23, 2007.

[32] Federal TANF law does not address the income of children, and most states disregard earnings for children (defined mostly as those under age 18 or 19) in school; however, some limit the time that their income does not count. This is based on a CRS review of the Urban Institute's Welfare Rules Database, April 2012, by Gene Falk, Specialist in Social Policy.

in the second half of 2009. Since that time, there is some evidence that GDP adjusted for inflation (real GDP) has increased, albeit unevenly, in each quarter since the third quarter of 2009.[33] The labor market, however, has not recovered despite recent economic growth. Since the start of the recession in December 2007 through December 2011, there was a net loss of approximately 5.8 million total jobs. Thus, despite recent growth in the economy, there has not been comparable recovery in the labor market.[34]

Firms are more likely to lay off those with less seniority because they have made fewer investments in these workers. Young people are often the first to be laid off. Firms may also stop hiring, which affects those who are looking for a job or entering the labor market. Unemployed youth, particularly teens, must then compete with experienced laid off adults for available jobs. For example, there was a slight *increase* in the labor force participation rate of individuals ages 55 and over, from 38.9% in the fourth quarter of 2007 to 40.4% in the fourth quarter of 2011.[35] In other words, one segment of the population that likely has significant labor market experience is not exiting the labor force but has instead increased its participation, which may make it more difficult for workers with less experience to compete.[36] Younger workers, on the other hand, seem to have become discouraged and have dropped out of the labor market altogether. For example, in the same period (fourth quarter of 2007 through the fourth quarter of 2011), the labor force participation rate for individuals ages 16 through 24 declined from 59.3% to 55.5%.[37] This decrease supports the earlier evidence that some youth have become discouraged and are dropping out of the labor force (albeit some youth may be opting to pursue education).

In contrast, good economic times operate to the relative advantage of young workers: when product demand is high and labor is in short supply, firms become more willing to hire those they consider less desirable, such as young inexperienced persons. Likewise, with better employment prospects, labor force participation could be expected to be higher. In the high-growth 1990s, for example, the youth labor force participation rate was in the 65% to 67% range.[38]

Experience and Education

Experience and education are also important determinants of the success of youth in the labor market. These factors are not specific to youth, of course, but may have a more pronounced effect on youth because of their relative lack of experience and education compared to other labor market participants. Further, the labor market trends for youth are associated with their relatively

---

[33] See CRS Report R41332, *Economic Recovery: Sustaining U.S. Economic Growth in a Post-Crisis Economy,* by Craig K. Elwell for a discussion of measuring decline and recovery in the most recent recession.

[34] Congressional Research Service (CRS), based on data from U.S. Department of Labor, Bureau of Labor Statistics, "Employment, Hours, and Earnings from the Current Employment Statistics Survey," http://data.bls.gov/pdq/querytool.jsp?survey=ce.

[35] Congressional Research Service (CRS), based on data from U.S. Department of Labor, Bureau of Labor Statistics, Current Population Survey; data are seasonally adjusted.

[36] Neeta P. Fogg and Paul E. Harrington, "Rising Demand for Older Workers Despite the Economic Recession: Accommodation and Universal Design for the New American Workforce," *Public Policy & Aging Report*, vol. 21, no. 2 (Winter 2011), pp. 11-13. This analysis shows that from December 2007 to December 2010, the rise in unemployment among workers 55 and older was countered by their increased entry into the labor market.

[37] Congressional Research Service (CRS), based on data from the U.S. Department of Labor, Bureau of Labor Statistics, Current Population Survey; data are seasonally adjusted.

[38] Ibid.

---

frequent job changes, with each transition potentially involving a spell of unemployment. About two-thirds of all job changes occur within the first 10 years of a young person's working life, during which time he or she will work for eight employers on average.[39] This initial period of frequent job turnover has positives and negatives. Frequent job turnover among new labor force members may reflect their trying out different positions and work environments until they find the optimal match; however, it may also reflect employer reluctance to hire inexperienced workers for career ladder positions and young workers in dead-end jobs having little reason to form a lasting attachment to any particular firm. Analyses of data from the National Longitudinal Survey of Youth (NLSY)[40] generally found that while typical young workers do not enter a long-term job (of at least three years duration) immediately after leaving school, they do by about age 22.[41] In a recession, a youth's short and disrupted work history may make hiring him or her less desirable.

Education also plays a role in whether youth seek and are able to find work. Youth may decide not to pursue employment and to attend school instead; they may want to do both, but may not have opportunities to work due to a lack of jobs. The rising rate of school enrollment has likely influenced the downward trend in the E/P ratio for teens and young adults. **Figure 6** shows that the rates of enrollment in higher education among 18- and 19-year olds and 20-through-24 year olds has steadily increased over time, reaching all time highs in 2009 (the most recent year available). That year, just under half of all teens ages 18 and 19 were attending colleges, universities, and professional schools—an increase of over 30% since 1970. Nearly 4 out of 10 young adults ages 20 through 24 were enrolled in higher education in 2009, compared to about 1 out of 5 in 1970.

---

[39] Jonathan R. Veum and Andrea B. Weiss, "Education and the Work Histories of Young Adults," *Monthly Labor Review*, April 1993, http://www.bls.gov/opub/mlr/1993/04/art2full.pdf.

[40] The NLSY is part of BLS' National Longitudinal Surveys program, which surveys cohorts of workers over time. The primary focus of the survey is on the employment experiences of respondents and other experiences related to employment, including education, training, marital status, fertility, participation in government assistance programs, income, and assets. The research discussed above and elsewhere in this report that references the NLSY is based on the 1979 cohort, who were ages 14-22 when the survey began. A somewhat younger group (ages 12-17) began to be surveyed in 1997.

[41] Julie A. Yates, "The Transition from School to Work: Education and Work Experiences," *Monthly Labor Review*, February 2005; and Jacob Alex Klerman and Lynn A. Karoly, "Young Men and the Transition to Stable Employment," *Monthly Labor Review*, August 1994.

Figure 6. Rate of College Enrollment Among Youth Ages 18-24, 1948-2009

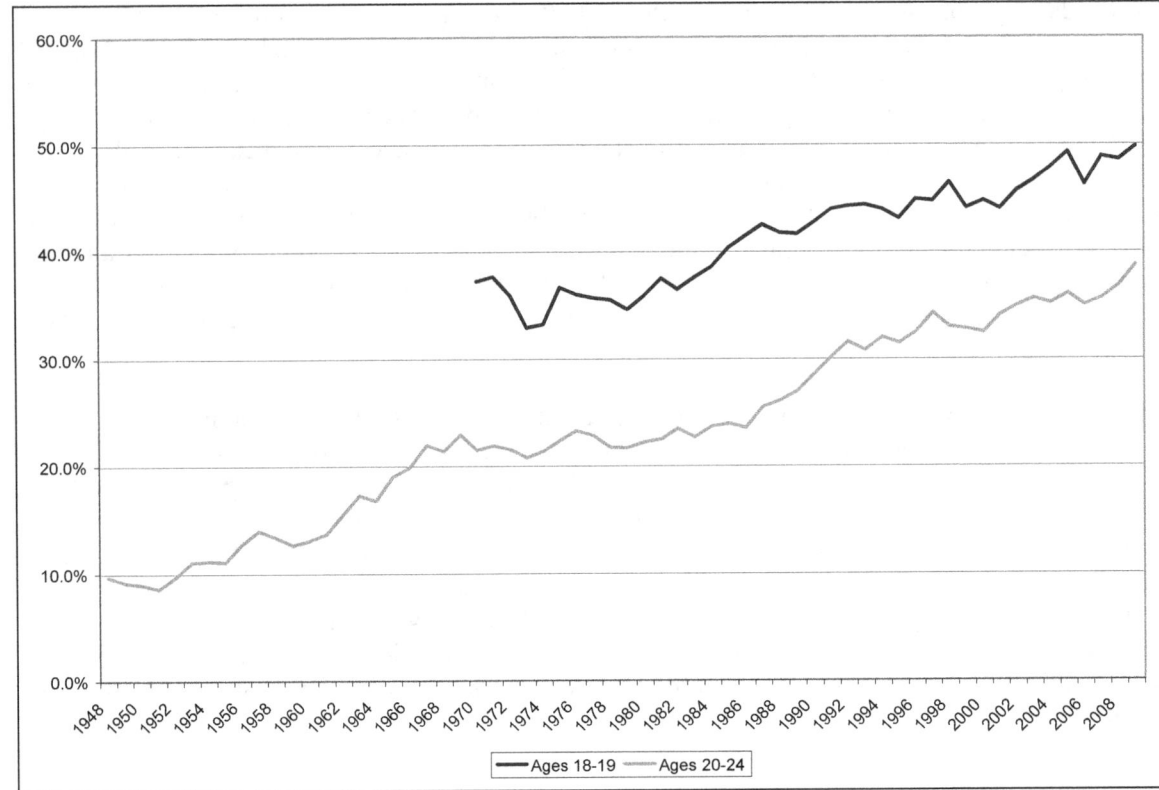

Source: U.S. Department of Education, National Center for Education Statistics (NCES), *Digest of Education Statistics: 2009*, "Table 7, Percentage of the Population 3 to 34 Years Old Enrolled in School, By Age Group: Selected Years, 1940 Through 2009."

Notes: College refers to public and private colleges, universities, and professional schools. The data for 18 and 19 year are not available prior to 1970.

A Department of Labor study attributes the declining summer teen employment beginning in the early 2000s to education.[42] The study found that the proportion of teens enrolled in school during the summer has steadily increased, from about 15% in 1985 to 53% in 2009. Teens appear to face greater academic demands and pressure, which may influence their education and employment choices. The study noted that more high school students are satisfying the requirements needed for attending a four-year college, and that a growing share of students are taking advanced placement (AP) courses. The average number of credits earned by high school graduates increased from 21.6 in 1982 to 26.7 in 2005. Also over this same period, the proportion of graduates who took an advanced mathematics course increased from 26.3% to 48.8% (the gains are similar for other advanced courses). Teens may feel compelled not to pursue work for the summer and instead opt for volunteer opportunities or internships in order to fulfill their graduation requirements and improve their prospects for getting into a four-year college or university. According to the study, Current Population Survey data from 2009 show that over one-quarter of teens ages 16 through 19 had reported volunteering at some time during the prior year.

---

[42] Theresa L. Morisi, "The early 2000s: A Period of Declining Summer Teen Employment Rates," U.S. Department of Labor, *Monthly Labor Review*, May 2010.

Young people may also forego working and pursue education instead because of the gains they can make in the labor market at a later time—although the extent to which this occurs is uncertain. Success in the workforce is related to education, with the payoff being lower unemployment and higher wages as educational attainment increases. **Figure 7** shows the unemployment rate and median weekly earnings for full-time workers age 25 and older in 2011. As the level of education rises, the unemployment rate decreases and median weekly earnings increase. Among adults with less than a high school degree, 14.1% were unemployed and earnings were $451 per week. This is compared to an unemployment rate of 9.4% and $638 in weekly earnings for a high school graduate. Adults with a bachelor's degree or higher had an unemployment rate of less than 5.0% and median weekly earnings that ranged from $1,053 to $1,665.

Figure 7. Median Weekly Earnings and Unemployment Rates by Education Level for Adults Age 25 and Over, 2011

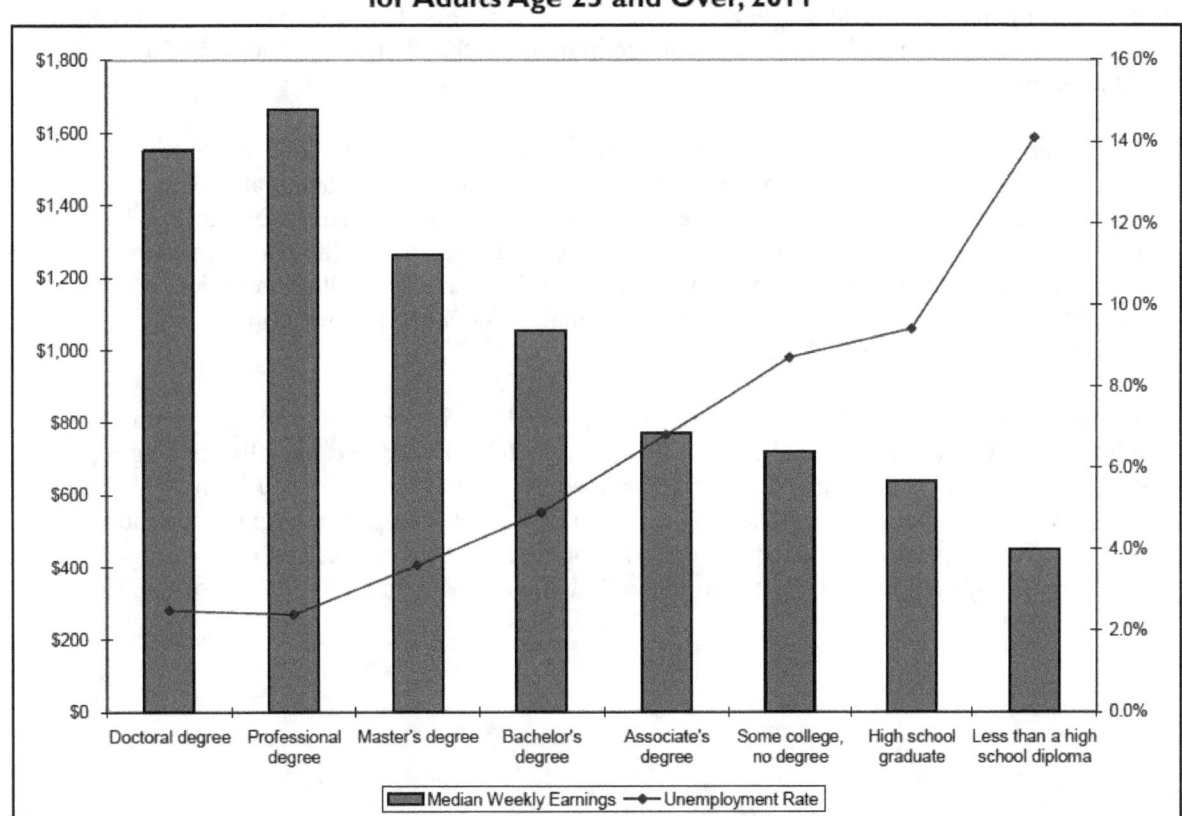

Source: Congressional Research Service (CRS), based on data from U.S. Department of Labor, Bureau of Labor Statistics, Current Population Survey. *Education Pays*, March 23, 2012.

Workers with higher levels of education are more likely to weather hard economic times.[43] According to a 2010 analysis, in the past two recessions, "the typical job loser was a high school-educated male in a blue collar job, such as manufacturing or construction, working in the middle of the country. In the past two recoveries, the typical job gainer was a female with a

---

[43] Anthony P. Carneval, Nicole Smith, and Jeff Strohl, *Jobs Wanted: Projections of Jobs and Education Requirements Through 2018*, Georgetown University, Center on Education and the Workforce, June 2010, http://www9.georgetown.edu/grad/gppi/hpi/cew/pdfs/FullReport.pdf.

postsecondary education who lived on either coast and worked in a service occupation—particularly healthcare, education, or business services."

Certain young people, minority males especially, are less likely to be employed in light of their relatively lower levels of education.[44] **Table 3** shows educational attainment by race and gender for young people ages 25 through 29 in three years: 2000, when the economy was expanding but youth employment was beginning a long-term decline; 2007, immediately before the start of the recent recession; and 2011, after the recession had officially ended. Data are available for all racial and ethnic groups, except Asian youth in 2000.

From 2000 to 2011, females made more significant gains in high school and college attainment than their male counterparts. In 2011, males and females were likely to complete high school at almost the same rate (86.7% for females and 89.4% for males); however, 36.1% of females had completed at least a bachelor's degree by age 30, compared to slightly more than one-quarter (28.4%) of the males. In nearly every racial and ethnic category, females were more likely than males to graduate from high school and college in both 2000 and 2011 (or 2007 and 2011 for Asian youth).

All racial and ethnic groups also experienced gains over time, except that the white female high school graduation rate decreased by less than a percentage point and black male college graduation rate decreased by 2 percentage points. In 2011, Hispanic males were far less likely to finish high school (69.2%) than white males (93.4%) and black males (87.6%); however 10% more Hispanic males received a high school degree in 2011 than in 2000. In addition, a relatively small share of black males (16.1%) and Hispanic males (9.6%) completed college in 2011, compared to white males (35.5%).

Data on Asian youth are available only for 2007 and 2011. A lower share of Asian youth graduated from high school or college in 2011 than in 2000. This was especially striking for Asian males, whose college attainment rate dropped from 59.8% to 51.5%. Still, in 2011 Asian young adults were about equally likely as white youth to have completed high school and more likely to have completed college or university: about half of Asian males and 61% of Asian females were college graduates, compared to about 36% of white males and 43% of white females.

---

[44] See CRS Report RL32871, *Youth: From Classroom to Workplace?*, by Linda Levine for a discussion of the role of gender, race/ethnicity, and other individual characteristics on youth labor force participation.

Table 3. Percentage of Young Adults Ages 25-29 Who Completed High School or College, by Gender and Race/Ethnicity: 2000, 2007, and 2011

Educational Attainment by Year	Total		Non-Hispanic White		Black		Hispanic		Asian[a]	
	Males	Females	Males	Females	Males	Females	Males	Females	Males	Females
High School										
2000	86.7%	89.4%	92.9%	95.9%	86.6%	85.3%	59.2%	66.4%	N/A	N/A
2007	84.9	89.1	92.7	94.2	87.0	87.8	60.5	70.7	95.8	98.5
2011	87.5	90.7	93.4	95.5	87.6	87.8	69.2	74.3	93.6	96.7
Absolute Change from 2000-2011 (Percentage Points)[b]	0.8	1.3	0.5	-0.4	1.0	2.5	10.0	7.9	-2.2	-1.8
Relative Change from 2000-2011 (Percent)[b]	0.9	1.5	0.5	-0.4	1.2	2.9	16.9	11.9	-2.3	-1.8
College										
2000	27.9	30.1	32.3	35.8	18.1	17.0	8.3	11.0	N/A	N/A
2007	26.3	33.0	31.9	39.2	17.9	19.9	8.6	15.4	59.8	62.0
2011	28.4	36.1	35.5	43.0	16.1	22.8	9.6	16.8	51.5	60.6
Absolute Change from 2000-2011 (Percentage Points)[b]	0.5	6.0	3.2	7.2	-2.0	5.8	1.3	5.8	-8.3	-1.4
Relative Change from 2000-2011 (Percent)[b]	1.8	19.9	9.9	20.1	-11.0	34.1	15.7	52.7	-13.9	-2.3

Source: Congressional Research Service (CRS), based on U.S. Department of Commerce, Census Bureau, Annual Social and Economic Supplement to the Current Population Survey, Table A-2, "Percent of People 25 Years and Over Who Have Completed High School or College, by Race, Hispanic Origin and Sex: Selected Years: 1940 to 2011."

Note: N/A means not available. College attainment refers to a bachelor's degree or higher.

a. The absolute and relative changes for Asian youth are based on 2007 and 2011 data since 2000 data are not available.

b. Absolute change refers to the percentage point change from 2000 to 2011 and is derived by subtracting 2011 data from 2000 data. Relative change refers to the percentage change over the same period and is derived by subtracting 2011 data from 2000 data and then dividing that number by the 2000 data.

Other Factors

The factors discussed thus far affect the labor market experiences of both youth and adults, although the effects tend to be larger for youth. There are additional factors that have been posited to have particular relevance for youth outcomes in the labor market.

Mobility

First, youth tend to have frequent movements in and out of the labor force. The educational calendar exacerbates the probability of unemployment for young labor force (re)entrants. They typically flood the labor market in May and June either searching for summer jobs after the school year has ended or seeking initial jobs upon graduating (or dropping out). While the regularly occurring swell in the labor supply of youth coincides with increased demand for workers in some seasonal industries, this is not the case for most firms in the economy.

Neighborhood Characteristics

Finally, other external factors can affect the labor status of young people. Among these factors are the characteristics of the neighborhoods in which they live, such as area employment and poverty rates, and proximity of those neighborhoods to jobs. An analysis that utilized data from the National Longitudinal Survey of Youth (NLSY) and U.S. census tract information for 1980 and 1990 estimated that 14-through-22 year olds who grew up in metropolitan areas with relatively high poverty rates had a lesser likelihood as adults of being employed in the civilian economy or in the Armed Forces and a greater likelihood of not being in the labor force.[45] Being raised in a poor neighborhood appears to more adversely affect young males, especially those in poor families, than females. Other research similarly shows neighborhood effects can vary according to the characteristics of youth. For example, another study based on NLSY data estimated that the adverse impact on labor market attachment of young out-of-school males living in disadvantaged metropolitan areas was harsher for those with less than 12 years of schooling.[46]

In addition to social isolation from work due to a dearth of role models and job referral networks, geographic isolation from fast-growing job-rich areas (i.e., spatial mismatch) has been shown to affect youths' employment outcomes. Some analyses estimated that limited social access has a more adverse impact than access to transportation. Nonetheless, the proximity of jobs was still found to affect their labor market involvement independent of other factors.[47]

Consequences of Youth Labor Force Participation Trends

The consequences of growing youth unemployment and decreasing E/P ratios among youth have not been fully explored in the research literature. The few recent studies that address the effects of youth labor market participation have focused on the individual outcomes for youth and not, for

---

[45] Steven R. Holloway and Stephen Mulherin, "The Effect of Adolescent Neighborhood Poverty on Adult Employment," *Journal of Urban Affairs*, vol. 26, no. 4 (June 2004).

[46] Bruce A. Weinberg, Patricia B. Reagan, and Jeffrey J. Yankow, "Do Neighborhoods Affect Hours Worked? Evidence from Longitudinal Data," *Journal of Labor Economics*, vol. 22, no. 4 (2004). (Hereinafter, Weinberg, Reagan, and Yankow, "Do Neighborhoods Affect Hours Worked? Evidence from Longitudinal Data.")

[47] See for example, Weinberg, Reagan, and Yankow, "Do Neighborhoods Affect Hours Worked? Evidence from Longitudinal Data;" Katherine M. O'Regan and John M. Quigley, "Where Youth Live: Economic Effects of Urban Space on Employment Prospects," *Urban Studies*, vol. 35, no. 7 (1998); and Steven Raphael, "Inter- and Intra-Ethnic Comparisons of the Central City-Suburban Youth Employment Differential," *Industrial & Labor Relationship Review*, vol. 51, no. 3 (April 1998).

example, on societal or economic outcomes such as reduced gross domestic product (GDP).[48] The studies found that on average, early youth unemployment has serious negative effects on income but not as strong of effects on future unemployment. Still, other studies show that youth entering the labor force during a downturn in the economy have poorer labor market outcomes in the long run.

Using data from the National Longitudinal Survey of Youth, researchers estimated the long-term effects of youth unemployment on labor market outcomes.[49] They examined the employment status of young men in the sample when they were in their 20s and later in their early 30s. They found that human capital (average level of education and training) increased over time, but also that early unemployment affected both wages and future unemployment. Their economic model projected that a six-month spell of unemployment at age 22 would result in an 8% lower wage rate, on average, one year later. The effects of this early spell persist; at age 26, wages would be 5% lower than what they would have otherwise been, and wages would be 2% to 3% lower at ages 30 and 31. Finally, the study found that past unemployment affected future unemployment, but only in the short term.

Studies of the effects of youth unemployment in OECD (Organisation for Economic Co-operation and Development) countries have found similar declines in wages as the result of early unemployment.[50] A study of youth unemployment in the United Kingdom determined that one year of unemployment at age 22 reduced wages by 13% to 21% 20 years later. The study controlled for education, family income, and personal characteristics. Another study found that unemployment immediately upon graduation from college is associated with substantial and permanent future earnings losses; however, the long-lasting effects of unemployment depend on the labor market conditions in which youth are unemployed.

Other research has examined how young workers fare when entering the labor market during a bad economy. One study used NLSY data to determine the effects of white males graduating from college with a bachelor's degree before, during, and after the recessions of the early 1980s (from 1979 through 1989).[51] The study examined how national and state unemployment influenced the wages, probability of being employed, and occupation type for these young men. After controlling for the possibility that individuals decide when to graduate from college in light of economic conditions, the study found that an increase in national unemployment by 1 percentage point decreased the wages of the general sample by about 4% in each of the 17 years following their graduation (relative to graduates who left school in 1989, when unemployment was at its lowest point during the 10-year period). In addition, higher unemployment in the year graduates

---

[48] At least one study, from the United Kingdom, has found evidence that spells of unemployment affect wages as well as non-labor market outcomes many years later. These other outcomes include happiness, job satisfaction, wages, and health. The study also found that youth unemployment involved significant social and economic costs. See David N.F. Bell and David G. Blanchflower, *What Should Be Done about Rising Unemployment in the U.K.?*, Institute for the Study of Labor, Discussion Paper No. 4040, February 2009, http://www.operationspaix net/sites/politiquessociales.net/IMG/pdf/dp4040.pdf.

[49] Thomas A. Mroz and Timothy H. Savage, "The Long-Term Effects of Youth Unemployment," *Journal of Human Resources*, vol. 41, no. 2 (Spring 2006), pp. 259-293.

[50] Stefano Scarpetta, Anne Sonnet, and Thomas Manfredi, *Rising Youth Unemployment During the Crisis: How to Prevent Negative Long-Term Consequences on a Generation?*, Organisation for Economic Co-operation and Development (OECD), OECD Social, Employment and Migration Papers, No. 106, April 14, 2010, pp. 14-17, http://www.oecd.org/document/49/0,3343,en_21571361_44315115_45008113_1_1_1_1,00 html.

[51] Lisa B. Kahn, *The Long-Term Labor Market Consequences of Graduating from College in a Bad Economy*, Yale School of Management, August 13, 2009.

left school was also associated with lower occupational prestige; however, the effects on the likelihood of being employed and on tenure were insignificant to modest. The analysis of state unemployment rates was more mixed but showed some long-term effects on wage and related labor outcomes.

The study also used Current Population Survey data to examine whether the recession of the early 1990s had similar impacts on workers. The CPS is a cross-sectional data set, and therefore the individuals in each annual survey vary. The study restricted the sample to white males with at least a bachelor's degree from 1997 through 2006, and found that a 1 percentage point increase in the national unemployment rate when these individuals were age 22 resulted in wage losses for 10 years; however, wage effects disappeared after 10 years. This could be due to measurement error because age 22 served as the proxy year for college graduation (which is unknown in the CPS) when, in fact, graduates may have finished college at a different age.

Similar research used the NLSY and CPS (Outgoing Rotation Group, ORG) to estimate the effects of white and black males graduating from college in a bad economy, except that this study also examined whether employers selected college graduates with the highest aptitude during a recession.[52] The study found that college graduates hired in a recession have, on average, higher abilities (based on the Armed Forces Qualification Test, or AFQT) compared to college graduates who enter the labor market in a good economy. Both the NLSY (1979 through 1989) and CPS (1979 through 1997) analyses showed, after accounting for a worker's aptitude, that wages declined by about 5% in the first three years of the worker's career. Workers sustained slightly lower wage losses in subsequent years.

Conclusion

This report provided an overview of the youth employment situation. It showed that over time, teen and young adults were less likely to be employed than older workers. This is likely the result of their relative lack of work experience, lower levels of education, and frequent movement in and out of the labor force. Perhaps most striking is that the youth employment rate, especially for teens, has eroded over the past decade—even in years when the economy was growing. The teen E/P ratio has been below 40% since 2002. This suggests a fairly recent long-term decline in teen employment, due to dismal employment prospects and youth withdrawing from the labor force to pursue educational opportunities. While the E/P ratio trend line for 20- to 24-year olds has been higher and more stable, the employment gains for this population have also been erased. At the start of the decade, the E/P ratio for young adults was about 72%, and by 2011 this rate dropped to 61%. Further, youth unemployment has been at its highest recorded levels recently. More than 3.4 million 16- to 24-year olds were unemployed in 2011. However, this figure does not reflect all young people who could be working if given the opportunity. Another 2 million youth in 2011 were out of the labor force but wanted a job. The American ethos that future generations can earn more and live more comfortably than their parents may be out of reach for many youth today. Additional research is needed on the effects of recent long-term youth unemployment. Such research could focus on how the current generation of young workers compares in terms of employment and wages to past generations of young workers who entered the labor force during downturns in the economy.

---

[52] Hani Mansour, *The Career Effects of Graduating From College in a Bad Economy: The Role of Workers' Ability*, University of Colorado, Denver and DIW Berlin, November 2009.

Appendix. Supplemental Tables and Figures

Table A-1. Labor Force Participation of Youth Ages 16-19 by Race and Ethnicity: 2000, 2007, and 2011

Numbers in thousands, not seasonally adjusted

	2000	2007	2011	Absolute Change from 2000-2011 (Percentage Points)[a]	Relative Change from 2000-2011 (Percentage)[a]
Labor Force Participation Rate					
All	52.0	41.3	34.1	-17.9	-34.4%
Male	52.8	41.1	33.7	-19.1	-36.2
Female	51.2	41.5	34.6	-20.8	-45.8
White	55.5	44.4	36.8	-18.7	-33.7
Black	39.4	30.3	24.9	-14.5	-36.8
Hispanic	46.3	37.1	28.3	-18.0	-38.9
Asian	35.8	59.7	21.7	-14.1	-39.4
E/P Ratio					
All	45.2	34.8	25.8	-19.7	-43.3
Male	45.4	33.9	24.6	-20.8	-45.8
Female	45.0	35.8	27.1	-17.9	-39.8
White	49.1	38.3	28.8	-20.3	-41.3
Black	29.8	21.4	14.7	-15.1	-50.7
Hispanic	38.6	30.4	19.5	-19.1	-49.5
Asian	30.7	56.4	16.2	-14.5	-47.2
Unemployment Rate					
All	13.1	15.7	24.4	11.3	86.3
Male	14.0	17.6	27.2	13.2	94.3
Female	12.1	13.8	21.7	9.6	79.3
White	11.4	13.9	21.7	10.3	90.4
Black	24.5	18.1	41.3	16.8	68.6
Hispanic	16.6	7.8	31.1	14.5	87.3
Asian	14.2	5.6	25.2	11.0	77.5

Source: Congressional Research Service (CRS), based on data from U.S. Department of Labor, Bureau of Labor Statistics, Current Population Survey.

Notes: The labor force participation rate is the percentage of individuals in the population who are employed and unemployed (those who are not employed and not looking for work are out of the labor force). Employment-population ratios represent the percentage of the non-institutionalized population who were employed. The unemployment rate is the percentage of individuals in the labor force who are jobless, looking for jobs, and available for work. Persons of Hispanic origin can be of any race and individuals of any race may be Hispanic.

a. Absolute change refers to the percentage point change from 2000 to 2011 and is derived by subtracting 2011 data from 2000 data. Relative change refers to the percentage change over the same period and is derived by subtracting 2011 data from 2000 data and then dividing that number by the 2000 data.

Table A-2. Labor Force Participation of Youth Ages 20-24 by Race and Ethnicity: 2000, 2007, and 2011

Numbers in thousands, not seasonally adjusted

	2000	2007	2011	Absolute Change from 2000-2011 (Percentage Points)[a]	Relative Change from 2000-2011 (Percentage)[a]
Labor Force Participation Rate					
All	77.8	74.4	71.3	-6.5	-8.4%
Male	82.6	78.7	74.7	-7.9	-9.6
Female	73.1	70.0	67.8	-5.3	-7.3
White	79.9	76.4	73.2	-6.7	-8.4
Black	71.8	68.3	66.5	-5.3	-7.4
Hispanic	78.2	74.8	72.0	-6.2	-7.9
Asian	63.0	59.7	55.1	-7.9	-12.5
E/P Ratio					
All	72.2	68.4	60.8	-11.4	-15.8
Male	76.6	71.7	63.0	-13.6	-17.8
Female	67.9	65.0	58.7	-9.2	-13.5
White	75.2	71.0	63.8	-11.4	-15.2
Black	61.0	57.9	49.7	-11.3	-18.5
Hispanic	72.4	69.0	60.7	-11.7	-16.2
Asian	58.6	56.4	49.1	-9.5	-16.2
Unemployment Rate					
All	7.2	8.2	14.6	7.4	102.8
Male	7.3	8.9	15.7	8.4	115.1
Female	7.1	7.3	13.4	6.3	88.7
White	5.9	7.0	12.8	6.9	116.9
Black	15.0	15.2	25.2	10.2	68.0
Hispanic	7.5	7.8	15.7	8.2	109.3
Asian	6.9	5.6	11.0	4.1	59.4

Source: Congressional Research Service (CRS), based on data from U.S. Department of Labor, Bureau of Labor Statistics, Current Population Survey.

Notes: The labor force participation rate is the percentage of individuals in the population who are employed and unemployed (those who are not employed and not looking for work are out of the labor force). Employment-population ratios represent the percentage of the non-institutionalized population who were employed. The unemployment rate is the percentage of individuals in the labor force who are jobless, looking for jobs, and available for work.

a.   Absolute change refers to the percentage point change from 2000 to 2011 and is derived by subtracting 2011 data from 2000 data. Relative change refers to the percentage change over the same period and is derived by subtracting 2011 data from 2000 data and then dividing that number by the 2000 data.

Figure A-1. Labor Force Trends for Youth Ages 16-19

Not seasonally adjusted

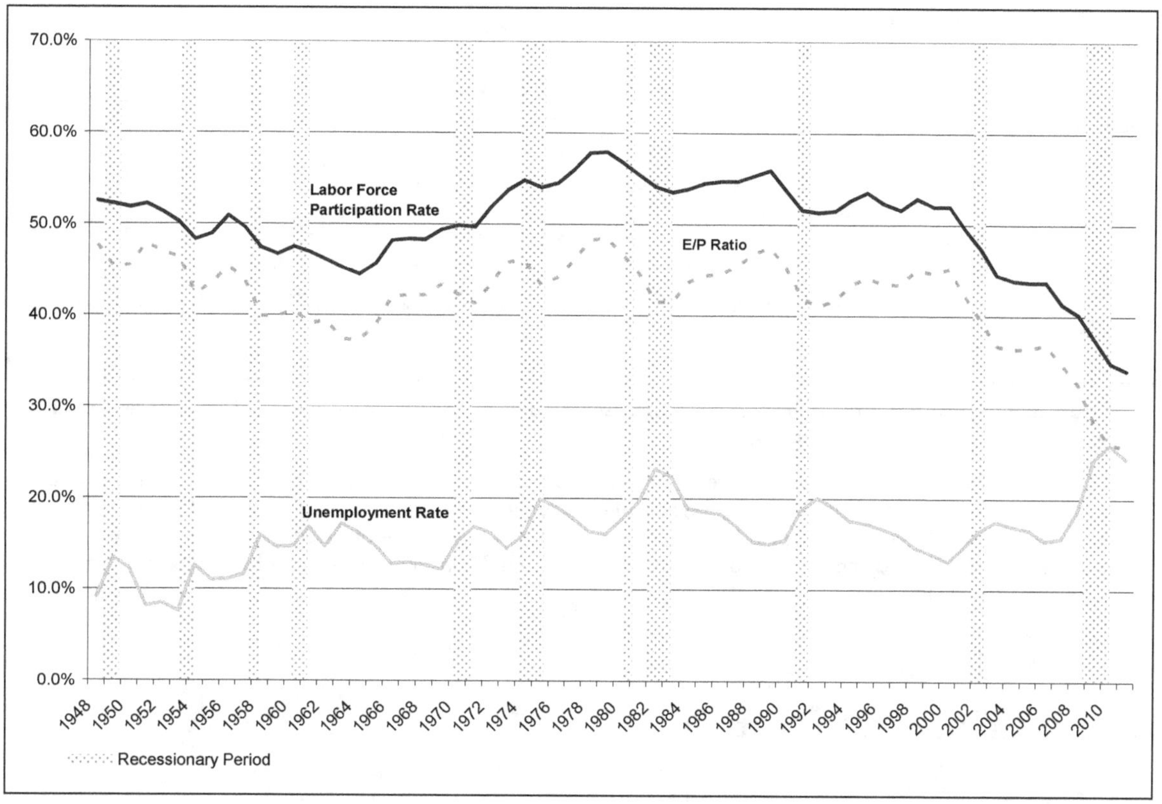

Source: Congressional Research Service (CRS), based on data from U.S. Department of Labor, Bureau of Labor Statistics, Current Population Survey,

Notes: The labor force participation rate is the percentage of individuals in the population who are employed and unemployed (those who are not employed and not looking for work are out of the labor force). Employment-population ratios represent the percentage of the non-institutionalized population who were employed. The unemployment rate is the percentage of individuals in the labor force who are jobless, looking for jobs, and available for work. Persons of Hispanic origin can be of any race and individuals of any race may be Hispanic.

Figure A-2. Labor Force Trends for Youth Ages 20-24
Not seasonally adjusted

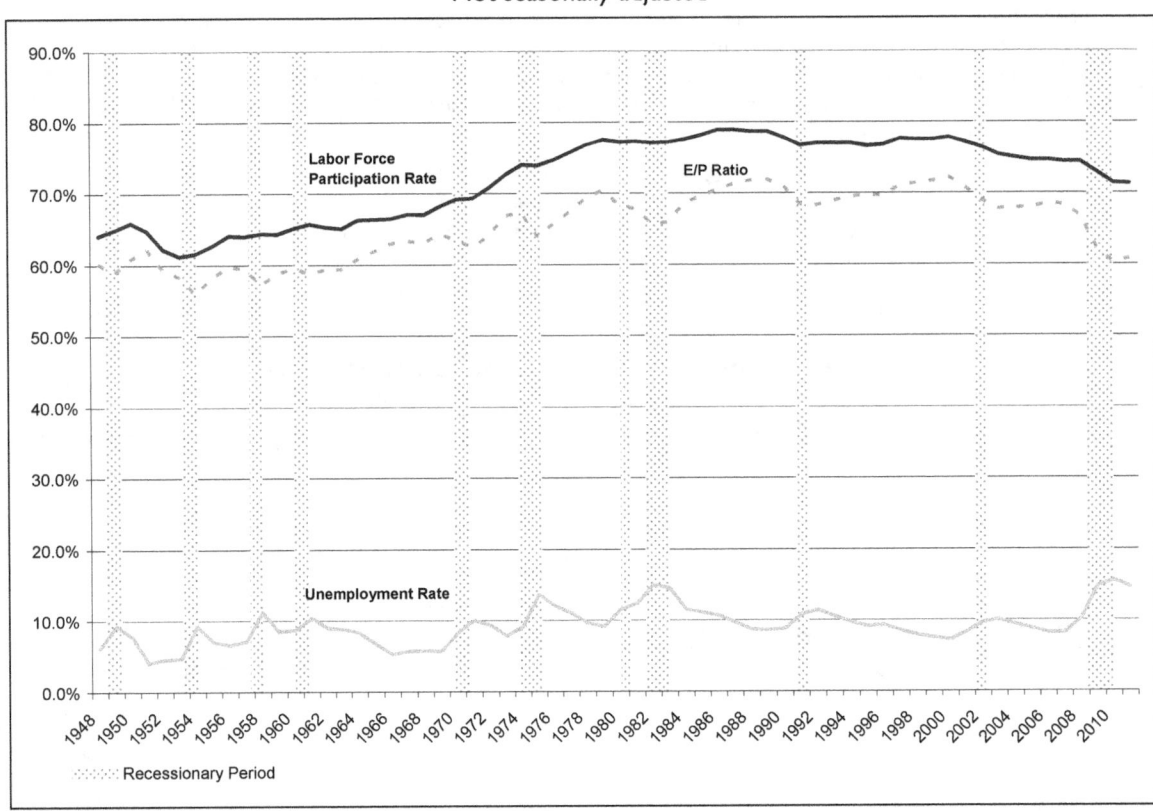

Source: Congressional Research Service (CRS), based on data from U.S. Department of Labor, Bureau of Labor Statistics, Current Population Survey,

Notes: The labor force participation rate is the percentage of individuals in the population who are employed and unemployed (those who are not employed and not looking for work are out of the labor force). Employment-population ratios represent the percentage of the non-institutionalized population who were employed. The unemployment rate is the percentage of individuals in the labor force who are jobless, looking for jobs, and available for work.

Author Contact Information

Adrienne L. Fernandes-Alcantara
Specialist in Social Policy
afernandes@crs.loc.gov, 7-9005

Acknowledgments

The author would like to thank colleagues David H. Bradley, Specialist in Labor Economics; Abigail B. Rudman, Information Research Specialist, Thomas Gabe, Specialist in Social Policy; and Gene Falk, Specialist in Social Policy, for their contributions to this report.

www.ingramcontent.com/pod-product-compliance
Lightning Source LLC
Chambersburg PA
CBHW081412170526
45166CB00010B/3314